Copyright © 2023 by Macloy Bros. Corporation

All rights reserved.

No portion of this book may be reproduced in any form without written permission from the publisher or author, except as permitted by U.S. copyright law.

Cover by Maceo K. Moore

Illustrations by Maceo K. Moore

Down in Prairie Dog Town

This Book Belong's To:

In the wide-open prairies of the Wild West, there lived a cute little prairie dog named Rodeo. Rodeo lived a good life with his family and friends, in a town called Prairie Dog Town.

Rodeo lived on a farm. Where his father, Paw Paw, grew food for the town.

His mother, Maw Maw, loved to cook and bake delicious meals with ingredients she grew on the farm. Rodeo's family always shared their food with everyone in Prairie Dog Town.

One day, something bad happened. A gang of bandits called the Hoot Gang, led by Creech, the Burrow Owl, destroyed Rodeo's town and took all the food they had!

All the prairie dogs were worried, but Rodeo didn't give up hope. He knew he had to do something to help his friends and family. So, he decided to go search and find the missing food.

FOOD BANK

Rodeo knew this journey was too big to do alone. He decided to ask his best friends to join him.

Rodeo went straight to his friend Prinkley's home. "Hey, Prinkley, I'm going on an adventure to find the missing food." Do you want to come?" Rodeo asked.

Prinkley thought about it for a moment and then her eyes lit up. "I'm in!" she said. "But we can't go without Fiddles," Prinkley suggested. Rodeo agreed, and the two of them went off to find Fiddles.

Rodeo and Prinkley went to their friend Fiddle's house and found him snacking on some sunflower seeds. "Hey Fiddles, we are going on an adventure!" Rodeo shouted. "What? An adventure where?" Fiddles exclaimed, looking up with a mouthful of sunflower seeds.

"I want to explore the wild west and find the missing food. Wouldn't it be awesome to be the town's heroes?" replied Rodeo. Fiddles was afraid to go, but Rodeo and Prinkley said "Come along it will be fun!"

After gathering his friends. Hoping to be successful, Rodeo went to his uncle Fuzzy's house for a wagon to bring all the town's food back.

Rodeo scurried up to the doorstep of his uncle Fuzzy's home. "Howdy, Uncle Fuzzy! Can I borrow your wagon for my adventure in the wild west?"

Uncle Fuzzy's fur shook with laughter as he smiled at his nephew. "My dear Rodeo, of course, you can! I will even let you use my jack rabbit old Floppers to pull it too.

But what kind of prairie dog goes on an adventure without supplies?" Rodeo's eyes widened as he realized he had forgotten about the important things. "You're right, Uncle Fuzzy. What do I need?"

"Well, you'll need a jar of pickles for when you get hungry on the trail, then a slingshot to launch rocks into the sky, and a trusty lasso to round up any varmints you come across! And don't forget to pack some cactus juice for those hot and dusty days," Uncle Fuzzy said.

Rodeo nodded gratefully. "Thank you, Uncle Fuzzy. You're the best!"

With his wagon full of supplies, Rodeo and his friends set off on their adventure to find the gang of bandits who took the town's food.

While traveling in the open plains of the Wild West, Rodeo and his friends traveled through bad terrain. It was filled with tall rocks and steep hills.

Fiddles was scared.
Rodeo turned to Prinkley and Fiddles and said, "I know this looks scary, but we can get through it if we work together."

"Rodeo is right; we can do this!" Prinkley cheered, as they continued their adventure.

Fiddle's stomach rumbled. "I'm hungry, and we're out of pickles!" Fiddles groaned. Rodeo turned to Fiddles and said, "There is a river up ahead; we can find some berries along the riverbank."

"GRRRr..."

"Okay..." Fiddles moaned.

Then suddenly, Fiddles spotted something in the distance. It looked like a plate of cookies. Fiddles loved cookies more than anything! He jumped out of the wagon and ran towards the plate of cookies.

FREE COOKIES

"SNAP!"

Rodeo and Prinkley turned around and saw Fiddles stuck in a trap.

"I got you now!" hissed Gold Fang. Gold Fang was a rattlesnake with one gold fang that was known for eating prairie dogs in the Wild West.

"We have to defeat Gold Fang and save Fiddles!" Rodeo exclaimed to Prinkley.

"But how do we do that?" Prinkley asked.
Rodeo rushed to his trunk of supplies and pulled out the slingshot.

"Okay, Prinkley, I will distract Gold Fang while you get Fiddles out of the trap," Rodeo said.

"I got it," Prinkley said, moving quietly to get Fiddles from the trap. Just as they were about to escape, Gold Fang caught sight of them.

"You won't get away from me that easily!" Gold Fang hissed, slithering towards them. But just as Gold Fang was about to strike, Rodeo stepped in front of him.

"Hey, over here! Come and get me!" Rodeo shouted, running in circles around Gold Fang.

While Gold Fang was distracted, Rodeo pulled back the slingshot and launched a rock at him. The stone hit Gold Fang in the head, knocking him out cold.

"We did it!" Fiddles shouted, jumping up and down with joy. "Thanks for saving me," Fiddles said to Rodeo and Prinkley. Before the gang continued their adventure, they took a break and ate the plate of cookies from the trap.

Finally, the little prairie dogs reached the hideout of the Hoot Gang where Creech and his band of outlaws lived.

Rodeo stayed calm and came up with a plan to sneak in and get the missing food.

The three prairie dogs were able to sneak into the gang's hideout. Inside, they saw the pile of food that was taken from Prairie Dog Town.

Rodeo and his friends made their way toward the food and put the food in a cart. Then, they pulled the cart out of the hideout. "The plan worked!" Prinkley shouted as they were leaving.

But Creech spotted them and began chasing after them.

"Get them!" Creech shouted to his gang.

With Creech and his gang hot on their tails. Rodeo, Prinkley, and Fiddles ran for their lives.

Rodeo reaches the edge of a cliff. Taking a deep breath, he makes a bold move and jumps into the river below.

Prinkley and Fiddles follow him and they disappear under the water.

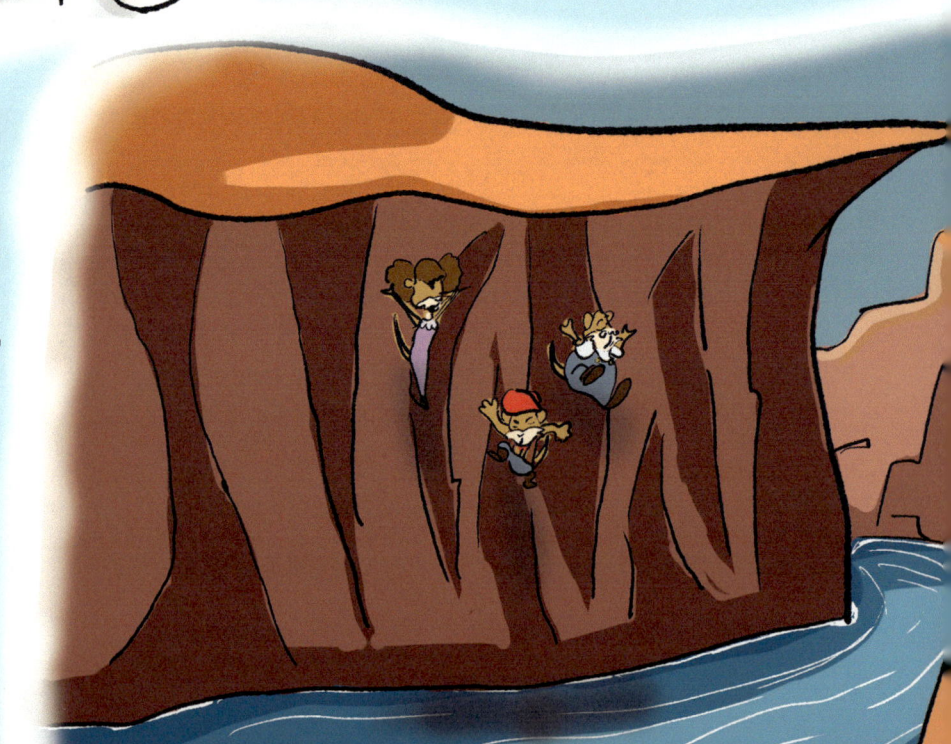

Creech and his gang search for them but could not find the little prairie dogs. Eventually, they gave up and returned to their hideout. "You little prairie dogs won't get away!" Creech screamed from the top of the cliff.

Rodeo and his friends came up from the water, soaking wet but happy. They successfully got back the missing food and outran the Hoot gang. "Hooray! We did it!" the prairie dogs chanted.

"Now let's go home with the food and be heroes!" Rodeo cheered.

As they return to Prairie Dog Town, they receive a warm welcome from the town.
Rodeo's parents ran to hug him.

"Where have you been, Rodeo?" Maw Maw asked.

"My friends and I traveled across the Wild West to find the missing food, and we found it!" Rodeo said, with joy.

"You are a brave little prairie dog, Rodeo." Paw Paw said.

The town Mayor gives the three little prairie dogs a gold badge for finding the food and saving the town. Rodeo and his friends are now known to be the bravest little heroes of the Wild West.

Prinkly	Rodeo	Fiddles
Paw Paw	Maw Maw	Uncle Fuzzy
Floppers	Gold Fang	Creech

Can you help Rodeo go through the maze to get the fruit basket?

Made in the USA
Columbia, SC
17 January 2024